HOW TO WRITE A BOOK

The Beginner's Guide To Writing A Nonfiction Book For Fun And Profit

KEITH EVERETT

CONTENTS

Introduction   v

1. Who Am I To Write A Book?   1
2. What Should I Write About?   11
3. Who Will Read My Book?   19
4. Creating A Great Outline For Your Book   28
5. Creating The Structure Of Your Book   37
6. Editing, Proofreading & Formatting   46
7. How To Create Your Book Blurb And Book   55
   Cover
8. Book Promotion Secrets   63

   Conclusion   73
   Sources   77

INTRODUCTION

Gone are the days when the only people who wrote books were the privileged few. Back then, you had to have the luxury of time and resources to spend months or years penning your manuscript, not knowing if it would ever be successful.

Now, everyone is at it, from your next-door neighbor to your great aunt. How come? Because nowadays, it's so easy, as long as you learn some basic dos and don'ts.

I bet that you have been pondering over writing your own nonfiction book for a long time, but keep putting it off because you didn't think you had what it takes. You may feel overwhelmed by the whole process, insecure about your writing skills, or just plain short of time. Many of you will feel confused about the publishing process, unaware of the fact that you can do it all from your computer or laptop. And then, I'm sure that a lot of you simply haven't decided on what subject to write about.

I'm here to tell you that EVERYONE is capable of writing and publishing a book and there are plenty of aids out there to help you. This book is one of them and it will take you through the whole process, from what to write about to how to get your first book published and generate sales. Yes, you can do it all.

You may be full of hesitation, wondering where to start, worried that no one will read it, not sure what costs are involved, or confused about how the marketing side of it works. There is a knack to it, just like anything else in life, but once you start, you will kick yourself for not doing it earlier.

When I wrote my first book, **MONEY MIND CRUSH**, I really had no idea what I was doing. Just like you, I wanted to get my skills and experience down on paper but had no clue where to start. I was baffled by the deluge of information on the internet, confused about some of the lingo bandied about, and felt as if I was preparing to climb Mt. Everest. There was nothing out there to give me a step-by-step guide to how to write, publish and promote a successful nonfiction book on Amazon.

We are all beginners at some point in our lives. It's easy to look back with hindsight once you've got the experience to say, "Oh, yeah, that's easy." But when you are starting off, you don't have that benefit. That's why having a trusty guide that will walk you through the whole process is a lot better than wasting hours of time, energy, and possibly money, making mistake after mistake, and feeling utterly frustrated.

That's why I decided to write this book because I know that a lot of you may be struggling with the same issues. There seem to be so many questions before you even kick off, and the answers are scattered throughout that infinite Google universe. It takes a lot of time to trawl through all of the blogs and articles online and even when you have done that, it's not until you sit down and start that you come up against problems you couldn't even have anticipated at the offset.

After my first book venture, I realized that it would have been super helpful if only I had some kind of handbook or manual to get me from *page 1* to *number 1 best seller* (I can dream...). Sure, there are some excellent online courses out there but they can be pretty expensive. If you are on a low budget, they aren't always an option. I did discover some useful books on the topic but they seemed quite complicated and intense for a novice like me.

I just wanted clear, concise, easy-to-follow advice on what to write, how to write it, and how to successfully self-publish.

That's why I have written this book.

In it, you will not only discover that there is at least one story in you, but also that you can navigate your way through all of the different stages from draft to bookshelf with confidence. It's not rocket science, but there are many tips and tricks that beginners just don't know about. I want to share them with you.

This book goes through all the basics of how to self-publish on Amazon. It also offers advice on marketing options and tools. As you go through each chapter, you will find useful guidance and handy hacks that will help you to achieve success with your first publication.

- We'll take a look at how to gain the confidence to actually begin writing, how to find topics to write about, and how to find your target audience.

- You'll learn about best practices, such as preparing your book outline and the importance of creating a sound structure.

- Then, we will dive into the world of editing, proofreading, and formatting your finished manuscript — the three stages that often baffle first-time writers the most.

- There's useful info on how to create a compelling book cover and where to find the best designers for the job.

- We'll go through how to write that perfect book 'blurb' and learn about making book descriptions that help to drive sales on Amazon.

- Finally, you will discover the many different ways to self-promote your book and get great reviews, something that authors are often completely in the dark about.

As I went through the whole self-publishing process for my first book, it was definitely a learning experience for me. I had been putting off writing a book for so many years and it wasn't until COVID-19 came along that I finally ran out of excuses. Now, I had the time to sit down and pursue my dream, but where to begin? I must admit that, at times, it felt like a real struggle and was often a case of trial and error. But I pushed on and persevered, motivated by the desire to complete something that I could be proud of. It was a truly rewarding experience and I'm now a multiple author, something that I wouldn't have believed if you told me a few years ago.

My real passion lies in helping others and if I can do that here, then mission accomplished.

I hope you enjoy completing and publishing your book, whatever your reasons for writing. Whether it's for fame, profit, the desire to offer self-help tips, to present something new to the world, or just to share your life skills and wisdom, knowing the 'why' is the secret to success.

Whatever your motivation may be, once you sit down to start writing, keep this book as your desktop assistant. When you get stuck or are losing momentum, remember that each chapter gives you a sound rung to stand on in the ladder to self-publishing your nonfiction work.

Once you are done, the sense of accomplishment at seeing YOUR book on Amazon is totally exhilarating and you will definitely feel like you have just conquered Mt. Everest. And who knows; it may even become a #1 bestseller!

Are you ready to go for it?

Great. It's time to sit down and begin.

❧ I ❧

WHO AM I TO WRITE A BOOK?

If you do a keyword search on Amazon for the term 'nonfiction', you will find well over 70,000 results. Within that category, there are multiple sub-genres, ranging from Arts & Photography to Memoirs, Crafts, and Hobbies such as Gardening. There are books out there on every subject under the sun but guess what; not all of them have been written by scientists, scholars, professional writers, or experts.

Books are Amazon's biggest category, currently listing about 44.2 million for sale on their website. They sell physical books as well as ebooks through their Kindle store and audiobooks on Audible. Although book sales represent less than 10% of Amazon's revenue today, that is still a massive number, adding to the annual income of $280 billion and rising.

Many of these books have been written by people just like you and me. Not all of the books for sale on Amazon about gardening have been published by horticultural experts or professional gardeners. Some of them have been penned by ordinary folk who simply have a passion for flowers or a penchant for home-grown spuds. What all these people have in common is a desire to publish their own work and the guts to go ahead and do it.

Since Amazon was launched 25 years ago, it has become the world's largest online retailer and has made it relatively easy for writers to self-publish their work on the platform. This growth didn't occur just because people like writing, but also because we still love buying books. Be it in traditional paperback format or as an audiobook, books are big business and there is something for everyone.

Once you have decided that writing and publishing a nonfiction book is something you wish to do, the next step is to convince yourself that you are capable of it. It can seem like an extremely daunting task at first, with questions popping up in your head such as:

Will it be good enough?

Will anyone read it?

What if I get bad reviews?

What if it doesn't sell?

All valid questions that we are going to tackle in this book, which you will see as you go through each chapter. The more stubborn worries that may prevent you from even starting are things like:

I've never written nonfiction before

I'm not a real writer

I'm not an expert on the subject

I'm not very good at writing

I'll never get it finished

The above bullet points can be real obstacles to sitting down to write and are often due to a lack of confidence, or are simply excuses not to get started. My take on that is: if you are reading this, then you really do want to write a book and simply need a little push to help you on your way. That's where I can help you.

What Is Nonfiction?

Let's take a look first at what we mean when we say, "I want to write nonfiction."

By definition, nonfiction is anything that intends to offer truth and accuracy about people, events, or information in general. It can be in the form of essays, biographies, memoirs, or informative work on any subject. You may write a self-help book on how to raise self-esteem or create a cookery book full of your granny's favorite recipes.

Nonfiction is usually seen as easier to write than fiction because it doesn't require any sophisticated literary techniques or skills. Of course, it has to make sense and be interesting or informative to the reader, but you don't need to have a degree in literature or be the next Ernest Hemingway/Emily Bronte. You just need to get across your chosen subject in a clear and appealing way.

You may have read several nonfiction books and, depending on the context, you can refer to them during your writing process to check how they are presented. Think about the type of language they use, the style, and how the information is laid out. This book is a great example of nonfiction, so use it as a model if you like and take as many tips from it as you need to.

. . .

WHAT IS A WRITER?

No one is a real writer until they begin to write. OK, some people do have a natural talent, but not everyone. Most of us are great storytellers though and have a lot to say. If you have an interest in, knowledge of, or experience with dogs, for example, you probably know more about them than the next person. I am sure you could talk for hours on the subject and if that's the case, you can also write down what you know.

Once you put your thoughts onto paper, or screen as is more often the case these days, then it's not a large leap to the next phase, which is getting your work published. That makes you a writer, or at least an author!

WHO IS AN EXPERT?

We are all experts on at least one thing, beginning with our own lives. Many people have made it into publishing by writing their autobiography or memoirs. One of the easiest ways to complete a book is to write what you know about and who is more qualified than you to tell your own life story? If you prefer to focus on your interests, hobbies, or skills, you don't need to be a member of a professional body or have won the Nobel prize first.

Think about what topic you want to focus on and if there are gaps in your knowledge, do the research. There is a wealth of information at your fingertips when you search online and as long as you use your own words, you can offer your readers an in-depth look at any subject you choose. Make it informative, factual, and interesting, and show off your expertise as you do so.

WHO IS GOOD AT WRITING?

If you can write a shopping list, you have the potential to write a nonfiction book. I know it sounds ridiculous, but it really is as simple as that. Your text may be poor, you might make a lot of spelling mistakes, or have awful grammar. Let me tell you now that you don't need to worry about that. There are expert editors and proofreaders out there who can turn your manuscript into something more readable. Clever AI software is also freely available nowadays to steer you in the right direction and we'll get to all of that in Chapter Six.

One way to improve your writing if you feel unsure of yourself is to read more. This is one of the untold secrets to being a good writer because the more you read, the more your brain picks up patterns of arranging text, how to spell words, and it enriches your vocabulary too. It doesn't have to be books: you can read newspapers, magazines, blogs, or online articles — anything that helps you to get a better grasp of what makes for decent writing. There are plenty of online writing workshops you can enroll in if you feel that you need a crash course and, eventually, you will develop your own style.

WHEN IS A BOOK FINISHED?

When you write your nonfiction book, you decide when it starts and when it finishes. There are no hard and fast rules about how many pages it must be, or how many words it needs to have. There are some general guidelines, depending on if you want to publish it as a paperback or also want to make an audio version, but we'll come back to that later.

All you need to know at the moment is that once you have decided on the topic, making a rough note of what you want to say in a list form is a good way to begin. You can use that later for your book outline with different chapters for each point, helping you to stay on track. It will also give you a goal to work towards and you can change it at any time, depending on what works and what doesn't.

People often assume that it's the writing of the book itself that is the main work. It isn't. There is a lot to do after that, such as editing, formatting, creating a book cover, publishing it, and then promoting it. But it all starts with a draft manuscript so concentrate on that before you worry about the next steps.

Getting started

If we were all controlled by our fears and insecurities, we would never get anything done. Assuming that you really want to write a nonfiction book and get it published, you need to overcome some common mental hurdles.

Here are my ten golden rules for getting into the right writing mindset:

1. First of all, remember that ALL writers fret about whether their book will be a hit or not. It's part and parcel of the whole process and worrying about it is often unavoidable. My advice to you is to write for yourself first and foremost. Sure, you have to have a target audience in mind, but try to imagine that you are your first reader and use that as your yardstick. If you are happy with the end result, then that's a great start.

2. You may be a shy, introverted kind of person who isn't used to putting themselves out there. No need to worry too much about that either when you begin writing because there will be plenty of time for you to get used to the idea. In any event, you may wish to remain anonymous, and can do so by choosing a pen name when you finally publish, which is a very common practice.

3. Maybe you are a perfectionist and never feel satisfied with what you have written. That's fine, but the longer you procrastinate due to your 'imperfections', the less likely it is that you will complete the task. The best way to handle this is to avoid re-reading or checking your work all of the time. Just get down what you want to say and when you have finished the first draft, leave it for a few days. Go back to it with a fresh, less critical eye and only make obvious changes, rather than being tempted to rewrite the whole book.

4. It's no good deciding to write about an unknown topic just because you think it may earn you a large profit. Of course, you can hire a ghostwriter to do that for you if that is the case (more about them later) but for the purpose of this book, we are talking about YOU doing the actual writing. With that in mind, write about something that you can confidently talk about; a subject that you can back up.

5. Once you have decided what to write about, set some time aside each day to work on it, or use your weekends if you have little free time during the week. It's very important to be disciplined, and you can set your own schedule — one hour a day, 2, 3... it's entirely up to you. A good incentive to get you writing is to set a completion date. Decide when you want to complete your manuscript before you get into the publishing side of things.

How long it will take you is the same as saying how long a piece of string is. Some people may set themselves a couple of months, while others give themselves a year. Again, there are no hard or fast rules here but setting a rough date will motivate you to keep at it when you feel like slacking off.

6. Choose a space where you can work uninterrupted and create an environment conducive to writing. If you have a home office, that's great, but we don't all have that luxury. Yet, you can set up a small workspace in the corner of your

living room or bedroom that you use only for writing. Make sure that you have a comfortable chair that supports your back and neck correctly, and put on your writer's hat whenever you sit on it. There are plenty of co-working spaces available now if you prefer to write alongside other people or you may like to take your laptop to your local park. It's up to you where you write, but try to be consistent.

7. Join a writing group or forum for fellow scribes. There are a lot of support groups on Facebook and other platforms such as Reddit where you will learn tips and tricks of the trade. You will also meet other writers who are just starting out like you, or who have more experience. Knowledge is power, so don't be afraid to ask questions — the other members can be a great support network as many of them will be in the same boat as you. It's also a good opportunity to find the encouragement that you need to continue towards your goals.

8. Choose your weapons wisely. You may prefer old school pen and paper to write with, which is fine. Just remember though, that as we now live in a digital world, those sheets of paper will need to be electronically transferred to a digital document. You may find this time-consuming and frustrating so my advice is to begin as you mean to go on and start writing on a word document or use Google docs. If you are not very au fait with the process, do some research first — there are thousands of YouTube videos with great instructions on how to create documents and make use of the different writing tools.

9. Don't be afraid of feedback. The thought of people criticizing your work may have put you off writing until now. The truth is that once your book is published, you can't control what people will say about it so it's a good idea to learn how to handle feedback from early on. Once you are ready to

share your manuscript with others, don't give it to friends and family if you can avoid it.

Their opinions will probably not be very objective and could even leave you feeling personally insulted. The best people to share your work with are seasoned writers/readers on your forum or social media group who will give you more constructive, honest feedback.

10. Believe in yourself. Whatever your dreams, goals, or motivation are when you decide to write and publish your nonfiction book, begin by having confidence in what you can do. Don't listen to the negative inner critic that tries to sabotage your positivity and stop focusing on what you don't know. Equip yourself with as much info as you can about your chosen subject, be prepared to learn new skills, and have a vision of how you want the final book to look. Stick with it and achieve what may seem at the moment like an impossible accomplishment. You can do it.

Thousands of people all over the world have written and successfully published their first book on Amazon. Many of them have then gone on to write a second and a third book, even earning a respectable income from book sales. They come from all backgrounds and ages, offering the world their insights and knowledge on every subject you can think of. There is a niche for everyone and everything, from How To Fix Your Electrical Appliances to The Secrets To Great Mediterranean Cooking.

You'll find books on hobbies, crafts, history, science, art, travel, as well as biographies, weird facts, and real-life adventures. A large number of them have been written by people you may see every day on your commute to work; on the train, metro or bus. Although you can't spot a writer by their appearance, you can be sure that they are all around us, thanks to the revolutionary way in which self-publishing has become so accessible.

Not every book can become a bestseller and there is a lot of competition out there, but that doesn't mean you shouldn't put your own book on the Amazon bookshelf. It may seem daunting in the beginning but the most important advice I can give you is to try it.

What have you got to lose?

❧ 2 ❧

WHAT SHOULD I WRITE ABOUT?

Once you take that leap of faith and decide to write a nonfiction book, it's a good idea to have a clear picture of what you want to write about. You may have a burning desire to share a topic very close to your heart, or could be unsure and lacking inspiration.

Usually, people want to write a book because they have something to say or are committed to sharing their knowledge, wisdom, or experience. Perhaps you want to offer insight into a problem that you have the answers to, such as how to increase eshop sales. You might be keen to tell the story of how you single-handedly rowed across the Atlantic, or give an account of life in 1920s Manchester. The list is endless of what you can write about and if you are having trouble deciding, then there is one question that you need to ask yourself.

WHY are you writing this book?

If you don't know the answer to this key question, you may feel a little bit lost at first.

Let's take a look and try to decide how you want to proceed from here on in.

WHY are you writing this book?

You may have always wanted to write a book but not sure why. It's important to clarify that from the onset because it will define everything that happens throughout the process. You need to think about what your motivation is as writing a book is not a simple task to undertake. It will use up your time, energy, and possibly even some of your finances. What is it that drives you to want to write and publish your book?

Is it for money, fame, status? If any of those are on your list, then I'm going to have to disappoint you. There is no guarantee that you will enjoy either when you eventually publish your book so they are definitely not good reasons to begin writing. Unless you have a crystal ball or an established following of thousands on your social media network, it's difficult to predict how well your book will do. Hopefully, it will do great, but you just can't be certain about that.

Of course, if the prospect of it being a best seller drives you on, that's perfectly fine, but start off with realistic expectations and you won't be disappointed. Whatever your reason is for writing a book, be it a personal desire or a professional move, as long as you know the 'why', that is great. This gives you a clear view of how to go about writing, publishing, and marketing it.

My experience has shown me that there are three kinds of first-time nonfiction writers wanting to publish on Amazon:

1. The person who sees it simply as a business move

2. The person who wants to share their passion or expertise with others

3. The person who simply loves writing

Some of these may overlap. For example, you may love writing about astrology and also want to make a business out of it. It could be that you are interested in sharing your knowledge about wine-making and aren't particularly interested in high sales or profits. Whatever your motivation for writing, it's absolutely fine as long as it comes from within. If it doesn't, you may find it difficult to complete more than a few chapters as you run out of steam or interest.

Writing a book is a bit like a marathon, but the only participant is you. You need to be able to establish your own pace, set your own personal record, and find the energy to keep going. Therefore, the WHY is super important.

Now, deciding on what to write can often be tricky. In my **Awesome Kindle Book Ideas**, I talked a lot about this subject and you can head over to Amazon and purchase it now if you haven't already done so. If your mind is a blank, there are plenty of ways to find ideas on what to write about. You can begin by thinking about the following:

- What are your hobbies and interests?

- What or who inspires you?

- What do you do for a living?

- What kind of personality do you have?

- What are you good at?

Make a list of things that define and motivate you. When you have done that, consider which aspects you feel that you can write a book about. Do you have any great stories to tell, unusual experiences, or unique talents that would make for great reading?

How old are you? Do you want to share a specific skill or advice with others in your age bracket? Do you know someone else who you would like to write about; a family member or friend?

I met a young woman in her early 30s who had a sister with autism. She wanted to write a book for others experiencing the same problem so that they would know how to handle the situation. It was a very cool idea: she had both the personal experience and the motivation. She wasn't an 'expert' on the subject by any means but was prepared to do her homework and offer sound, practical advice. Can you write something similar based on your life experience?

Like I said earlier on in this book, everyone has a story to tell, or is good at something. You can write about whatever you like but first, you need to pin down what that is.

Search the internet

There are many ways to find topics to write about.

→ You can begin by going to the Amazon website book section and selecting the category 'Best Sellers and More'. Afterward, click on Print Books and a side menu will come up, revealing a range of categories from Social Sciences to Sports & Outdoors. Select a category that sparks your interest, such as Crafts, Hobbies & Home, and even more subgenres will come up, like Antiques & Collectibles, for instance. Once again, you will find a range of subcategories including topics like Coins & Metals. There are so many options covering all kinds of interests.

→ If you don't find something that appeals to you, that's fine. You can try a different search category. This will give you ideas about what to write about and you will also see which books have already been published on the specific subject.

◆ Open Google Chrome Incognito Browser. This stops Amazon from showing results based on your account information or search history.

◆ Select 'Books' for search categories

◆ Type in words or phrases relevant to your interests. Amazon will make suggestions as you type.

◆ Once you have finished your search, make a note of any keywords that come up. You can narrow them down even further, and discover what kind of books people are interested in buying on Amazon.

→ Check out your competition by searching the Amazon Best Seller Rank (ABSR). Each book has a specific ABSR number that is awarded once the item has had at least one sale. For that reason, the ABSR is a very good indicator of how well a particular product is currently selling on Amazon. The lower the product's BSR, the better it is selling.

→ If most of the books listed in the top 5 rank at #10,000 or better, it will be more difficult for you to compete with them. Equally, if these top 5 books have a lot of reviews, it means that you will have to do better than that if you want to get to their level of readership. This is no easy feat, so it may be worth avoiding this niche altogether.

→ If you are competing with a very established author or someone with a large following, my advice is not to try to get into that niche because it will be virtually impossible to achieve the success that you desire.

The most popular-selling nonfiction books on Amazon belong to the categories of **money, success, happiness, relationships**, and **dieting**. That may seem quite general but within each niche, there are thousands of smaller micro-niches. We can begin breaking the above down like this:

1. Business & Money

2. Politics & Social Sciences

3. Education & Teaching

4. Self-Help

5. Religion & Spirituality

6. Parenting & Relationships

7. Biographies & Memoirs

8. Crafts, Hobbies & Home

9. Health, Fitness & Dieting

10. Cook Books, Food & Wine

If you want to write a book about relationships, narrow the subject down even further and think about the content. You may decide to write about how to plan the perfect wedding. Do your research and see what other books are already out there on the subject. Then refine your topic even more, perhaps focusing on destination weddings only, or weddings for the over 50s.

The more specific it is, the greater your chances of attracting an audience. If there are already thousands of similar books on Amazon, why would anyone want to buy yours? You need to ask these tough questions if you want to have any kind of success.

Nonfiction books come in all shapes and sizes, so there is a lot of scope for writing something that will be worth reading. If you still find it difficult to decide what to write about, here are my top tips to give you more inspiration:

★ **Look at your own life.** What's your story? What challenges are you facing? What learning process are you going through right now? What is going on in your life?

★ **Look around you.** What are your family and friends up to? What about your family history? Any interesting characters/events that you could focus on? How about your home town and its past? Have any interesting things gone on there or are happening now?

★ **Future plans**. Have you got any projects on the back-burner that you intend to complete? Are they worth sharing with others? Thinking of building your own boat or opening a hair salon? Why not write about your trials and tribulations?

★ **Got a big idea?** Have you thought of an innovative new way to lose weight, discovered the secret to eternal youth, or got an idea about improving education that you want to share? We are all full of ideas and after doing some research, we may just have something to offer the world.

★ **List it!** People just love helpful lists, so why not list your top 50 restaurants and eateries in the area, the top 20 gyms, or the top 100 ways to cook pasta? How about making lists based on age group, interests, or geographical locations?

★ **Picture book.** You can publish your collection of fantastic photos from your travels, or highlight the wildlife in your area, with a description for each one. How about a walk through the history of your hometown, with your own photos highlighting its intriguing past?

★ **Letters or conversations.** Had any conversations with famous or influential people that you would like to share? Perhaps you have personal anecdotes about your time in the army or life in an ashram that would make for revealing reading.

★ **Are you a blogger?** Why not compile your best blogs in a book, centering on a specific theme? Maybe you have already written something and can expand on that. It could be your own personal journal or diary, which others may find inspiring.

★ **Love cooking?** How about sharing your recipes, or your granny's, for that matter? Are you a foodie who loves to try out new healthy products or exotic ingredients? Why not take it to the next level and write a book about it!

★ **Love life?** Share your ups and downs in the dating game, giving advice on what and what not to do. Spill the beans, but probably best to change all actual names, just in case...

★ **Self-help for others.** Can you help someone to overcome an eating disorder, or give advice on how to save money? A lot of people are looking for answers and maybe you can help!

★ **Express yourself.** Want to talk about politics, world peace, or religion? Join the global debate with your views on the subjects and bring something unique to the table using well-researched arguments and insights.

This list is by no means finite. There are so many things to write about and the world is your audience. Do your keyword research, look at what people are buying and listen in on different forums to see where there is a space for your book. You will come up with something eventually and if you change your mind and decide to write about something else instead, that is perfectly fine too.

❦ 3 ❧

WHO WILL READ MY BOOK?

The next big question that you have to ask yourself is:

WHO IS IT FOR?

Are you writing for your own pleasure, for a catchment group, or for the whole world? You need to know, because if you don't, how can you promote your book?

The best way to approach this is to have a **target group or audience** in mind from the offset. Think about who will find your book interesting enough to buy it. Let's say you want to write about your long career in hotel management. Who is more likely to be interested in that? What age group, gender or background are we talking about? Knowing this will help you to focus on making sure your book not only offers the right information but also that it is written in an appropriate style. Then, when it comes to promoting it, you will know where to direct your marketing strategy.

It may be tempting to imagine that the wider you cast your net, the better, but this is a mistake. The narrower your definition of 'reader', the more effective your marketing campaign will be. Remember that nonfiction usually slots into a specific subgenre, so writing for the whole world is a bit like throwing bait into the whole ocean and seeing what bites. You will have much better luck if you focus on fishing in a smaller area, like a river or lake.

Take the hotel management book, for example. If you believe it is going to appeal to all ages or backgrounds, then you are in serious trouble. Only those who have a genuine interest in the topic will be willing to buy the book. They may be of a certain age range, say 25-50, and could be new to the industry or even veterans themselves. Once you narrow it down, there is less chance that you will feel the need to go off on a tangent or include information that is already common knowledge to those in the know.

Your book will be much better for it when you establish your target audience. Identifying that group of people who will be entertained or helped by your book is crucial and it's for them that you are writing. But how do you find them?

1. Define your genre

The first step is to actually define what genre your book is. We know that it is in the nonfiction category, but there are hundreds of genres and subgenres for nonfiction books – which one is yours?

Let's say your book is about healthy living. Narrowing it down, it could look something like this:

Nonfiction > healthy living > daily exercise routine > sports injuries.

The more you fine-tune the content, the closer you are to establishing your target audience. If it's to do with sports injuries, you will help readers to find it easier when browsing. If you simply place it in the 'healthy living' section, that is too broad a genre for you to stand out. Remember that most people are looking for something quite specific because they want help in dealing with their problems.

2. Check out your neighbors

What other books are available similar to yours? Who is buying them and what kind of reviews are they getting? Have they been featured anywhere else, such as in blogs or book reviews? This will give you a deeper understanding of how to target the right audience for your book.

3. Create a reader profile

Imagine who your ideal reader would be and create a profile that will get you to really target your audience. Think about things like:

• Their age

• Gender

• What they do for a living

• If they are single, married, divorced, looking for love...

• Their education level: high school diploma or Ph.D.?

• Their geographical location

• Their income bracket

• What media they use (newspapers, online blogs, scientific articles)

• What social media they follow (Instagram, Facebook, Youtube)

- Their favorite activities/likes and preferences

- What problems they have

- What aspects of their life or lifestyle they wish to change

Imagine that you want to write a book on how to train puppies. You've worked in a dog rescue shelter in the past and have fostered several puppies until they found forever homes. You have built up a good skill set and realize that many people don't know what techniques should be used to raise well-behaved, happy dogs.

Your ideal reader, let's call him Dave, may be 30 years old, is a single male, works in IT, has a Bachelor's degree in Computer Programming, and lives in Cheshire. He may have an average income, reads online blogs, and watches Youtube videos. He loves dogs and is thinking of adopting a puppy that he can train as a guard dog. His problem is that he knows nothing about what is involved in puppy training and needs some practical tips and advice.

Dave could be your ideal reader and now you know who you are writing for. Your puppy training guide will be a hit with Dave!

4. Check your social network

Who is in your network at the moment? Do you have friends or colleagues who come to you for advice? What common interests do you share and how much time do you spend helping them with their problems? These are the kind of people who would probably buy your book. What about your social media followers? Who are they and why are they following you? What sort of feedback do you get when you upload a puppy pic or a useful tip? All of this is great background information to help you pinpoint your target audience

5. Dig deeper

Ask your network if they would be interested in a book about puppy training (or whatever it is you wish to write about). Be creative and engage people — everyone loves to air their opinion, especially on social media. Ask what problems they have come across, what tools they would like to have. If you haven't yet established exactly what you want to write about, ask people to give you three ideas, what they are interested in, what problems they face that they would like answers to.

Ask them what kind of books they are into and what they have read recently. Would they buy your book?

This market research will not only help you to nail down the topic that you will write about but will also determine everything from how you present it to the way you promote it. Identifying your target audience doesn't mean that no one else will buy your book. It just helps you to focus on the right readers who are most likely to search for and purchase a copy.

There are some other very good reasons why knowing who will buy your book will help you to write a better one.

They will help you to create a book that appeals to the right audience and enable you to promote it in the most beneficial way. Some things to consider are:

Is it adult content?

Age is one of the first things you need to consider when creating your content and will determine all aspects of your publishing journey. The children's book market is something entirely different from the adult or young adult one, so it's obvious that you need to have a fixed idea about who your book is suitable for.

Is it for the layperson or the seasoned professional?

If your book is about Quantum Physics, the chances are that the people interested in reading it will be those with a certain level of knowledge on the subject. Stephen Hawking may have created a best seller with his '*A Brief History of Time*', but that is because he wrote it in such a way that the average man on the street could understand it. If you can't do that, don't expect him to purchase it and read it.

Are you speaking to your reader in their language?

To write for an audience, you need to speak their language. It's one thing to write for the TikTok millennials and quite another to write for the baby boomer generation. They both live in slightly different worlds and don't always use the same language. Understand the trends and use words and phrases that reflect that or your reader will feel alienated and disinterested.

Size does matter

I hate to say this, but the size of your book does matter. Depending on your target audience, they can be either put off by a 400-page book on cycling or prefer it if it's a memoir. If you have written 90,000 words, it may be too big to be appealing to the person who is going to buy it. And don't forget: pricing is important and it's crucial that you set your book at a price compatible with your market.

You may feel that your 400-page book should be listed at the high-end of the price range because of all the hard work and time you have put into it. But if your competitor is selling something pretty similar at the lower end of the price scale, which one would you buy?

Know how to find or attract your target audience

It's a good idea to build some kind of following before your book goes to press, so you have a ready-made audience. You may have a good idea of who your target audience is now, but don't know where to find them. I created a Facebook page before the release of my first book and invited my friends and acquaintances to join. I reached out to fellow writers from various platforms and invited them to follow my page. Some did, and some didn't, which is natural because you can't expect everyone to jump on board.

Who uses social media?

Facebook is still the most popular social network in the world, with nearly 200 million active users in the US. About half of Facebook users belong to a Facebook Group, which is great if you are an author because you can set up an Author's Page or Group. To do so, click the + symbol in the upper-right corner of your Facebook account and select which one you want. An Authors Page allows you to write posts, add photos and videos. Fans can't post content on your page, but they can like and follow posts. A Facebook Group lets followers post their own content, but you will have to act as moderator, which can be time-consuming.

Instagram has 120 million active users in the US, 70% of whom are under 35, split roughly into 50-50 male and female, and user engagement is massive. It does require some time and effort to keep your Instagram account relevant because it is very much a 'here today, gone tomorrow' culture. You will need to be active regularly if you want to retain followers, making posts and stories on a daily basis if you can.

Instagram does involve a lot of 'following' of other people first if you want to build up your own fans and you can even tag like-minded people in your posts or share their content on your own page to get them to follow you back.

Twitter may have fewer active users than the other social media platforms but it does have a dedicated user base of 68 million in the US, 62% of whom are male. Many writers prefer it as it focuses more on the written word than on visual cues and it is a good place to establish yourself if your target audience uses it. Retweet posts and as you do so, connect with their followers in order to enlarge your circle.

Pinterest may not seem like an obvious choice, but it is one of the largest image-sharing platforms, with about 100 million users in the US. 30.4% of them are women aged 25-34 so if that's your target audience, it may be worth looking into.

Start creating engaging content for your audience on your chosen platforms and figure out the right time of day to share it with them. You can use software such as Hootsuite or Buffer to generate previously prepared content, which also helps you to track views and engagements. You will be able to keep a tally of how much interest you are getting and can try out different scheduling strategies until you get the maximum exposure.

Being active on social media is one way to attract even more followers and creates the right environment for you to target the people you want to sell your book to. There are also many groups, associations, and forums you can join to bring you greater exposure, and being part of a community is a great way to promote your book and reach out to your target audience.

A word of warning

Don't go overboard by just promoting your book, because it will become boring for your followers. Add interesting blogs, useful insights, or even funny memes and promote other books too that may be relevant.

The best ratio to work with is 80% relevant information and only 20% about your upcoming book. Generating a buzz is key, but you shouldn't make it seem like you are a pushy door-to-door salesman. People don't want to feel that they are simply consumers, so make sure that you offer fun, interesting, and relevant content on all of your chosen platforms.

❧ 4 ❧

CREATING A GREAT OUTLINE
FOR YOUR BOOK

Now that you know what you want to write about (hopefully), it's time to get down to the nuts and bolts of planning your book. You may feel that this is the most difficult stage of all because, although you have a lot of ideas about what you want to say, they are randomly scattered in your brain. That's why you really need to create a great outline.

A book outline is similar to a journey that you plan on your sat nav: it gives you the starting point, shows you which streets, towns, or cities you will be traveling through, and knows what your final destination is. It's like a roadmap to prevent you from getting lost and will navigate you through the whole book writing process.

With a good book outline, you will be able to write more quickly, follow a solid structure, avoid that annoying blank page syndrome, know in which direction you are heading, and eventually, produce your first draft.

Writing nonfiction needs a specific kind of outline, as opposed to fiction, which requires a very different approach.

In your nonfiction book, you need to have clearly defined content that is easy to follow and has a logical structure. This helps the reader to know how your book should be read and even how it should be heard if you intend to publish an audiobook. Most importantly, it helps YOU to gather your thoughts, stay on track, and prevent procrastination or writer's block.

After writing a few nonfiction books myself, I have learned what common mistakes a newbie writer can make, because I have made them myself. After going through that process and doing a lot of research on 'best practices', I have devised **five bulletproof steps** that you can take to make a good outline. This will help keep you motivated to produce a great book that people will enjoy reading. I'm going to show you how to create your outline, as well as explain what else to include for a complete Table of Contents.

Five bulletproof steps to create your book outline:

Most top-selling nonfiction books follow a certain format and once you begin to apply it, writing the actual content itself will become a lot easier. After a while, you may develop your own particular outline style, but there are still certain basics that you should follow to get the job done, once you have the idea for your book.

- Brainstorm your content

- Create your Table of Contents

- Summarize each chapter

- Breakdown your chapters into sub-chapters

- Choose your front and back content

1. Brainstorming your content

Brainstorming is basically an opportunity to get all of your thoughts down on paper so that you can begin to put them in some kind of order. There are many ways to do this (some of them more complicated than others), but I like to use the **5W** technique, which is a simple, effective way to get your creative juices working. You have your book idea and that's where you start. Take a sheet of paper and write down one line to describe your book or even a working title that you have in mind. Then, begin to ask the following questions, making notes of your answers:

❖ **What?** What is the concept or topic? Is it a self-help manual or a 'How to...' kind of book? What kind of things do you want to include?

❖ **When?** Is it time-specific? Is it a historical account or a contemporary comment on modern-day problems?

❖ **Who?** Who is it written for? Remember that identifying your target audience is essential.

❖ **Why?** Why is your book worth reading? What will the audience get out of it? What can you offer them?

❖ **Where?** Where can your ideas be applied? In which context will it be useful?

By answering the above questions on your sheet of paper, you are already beginning to build your content, which you will expand on later. It only takes a few minutes to do this, and you don't need to include a lot of elaborate details just yet.

2. Create your Table of Contents (TOC)

Begin by including an Introduction, which will present the topic.

Then, follow that with a list of chapter titles. For example, let's say that your book is about ways to set up a home business. Your first chapter may talk about the benefits of doing so and the following chapters can begin to give more practical tips, such as how to work efficiently, how to keep running costs down, and so on.

Once you have formed a series of chapter titles (which you can always change at a later stage), list them in your Table of Contents as Chapter 1, Chapter 2, and so on.

End with a Conclusion or Closing Chapter, in which you will wrap up your book, giving a summary of the main themes mentioned.

3. Summarize each chapter

After that, think about what the purpose of each chapter is. This should be a short summary of the main point you wish to make, and shouldn't be more than a couple of sentences. Here's an example of how it may look when you are done:

Introduction: *Ways to Set Up A Successful Home Business*

Chapter 1: *How Easy Is It To Set Up A Home Business?*

The types of home businesses, what skills are needed, and how to go it alone.

Chapter 2: *What Are The Hidden Costs?*

The amount of capital needed to start up a home business and the kinds of overheads to expect as a self-employed person or small company.

Chapter 3: *Setting Up An E-Shop Or Online Business*

The pros and cons of e-shops/retail businesses and how to do effective research on what sells online.

Chapter 4: *5 Ways To Attract Financial Investment*

How to understand what type of financial help is available and find investors/banks to fund your business.

Chapter 5: *Does Home Really Mean Home?*

What you will need to work from home and alternative solutions such as co-working spaces, as well as other options.

Chapter 6: *How To Market Your Service/Product*

Ways to upgrade your marketing skills and tips on how to gain wider exposure at less cost.

Chapter 7: *Planning Ahead*

Strategies for expanding your home business, employing extra staff, and broadening your product range or services.

Conclusion: *Are you ready to make the move?*

As you can see, each chapter pinpoints a certain aspect of the book that you want to talk about and its purpose in only a few words. This framework will help you to move through the book knowing exactly what to write, expanding on your ideas in each chapter.

4. Breakdown your chapters into sub-chapters

Now that you know what each chapter will be about, you can add extra information that you aim to include to each one. A good working plan will look like this:

Chapter 1: *How Easy Is It To Set Up A Home Business?*

• *Chapter Purpose: The types of home businesses, what skills are needed, and how to go it alone.*

• *Chapter Content:*

a. The types of home businesses

b. The ins and outs of setting up a home business on your own.

c. What skills are needed

d. How to go it alone

e. Shifting from employed to self-employed status

f. Obstacles and aids to your success

• *Key Takeaway: While the thought of setting up your own business from home may seem daunting, there are many ways to approach it and establish a successful business on your own.*

• *Recap of chapter and transition to next one: Now that you have learned about how easy it is to set up your home business, we will take a look in the next chapter at what kinds of costs may be involved to get you started.*

You can follow this structure for each chapter. As you do so, your mind will be working hard, bringing up lots of information that you want to share in your book. By getting those ideas down now, you have a fantastic model to work with and all that is left to do is expand on them in more detail.

5. Choose the front and back page content for your book

No outline is complete without your front and back page content. This is any extra information that you wish to include at the beginning of the book or the end. You don't have to worry about writing these until you have finished the main body of your book.

The **front content** should include the following and some of them are optional, while others are mandatory if you want to achieve a professional result. They include:

• Testimonials page or pages (optional). If you don't have any, not to worry.

- Title page (mandatory). Don't forget to include your author name.

- Copyright page (mandatory). If you don't have one, you can find many free templates available online to download.

- Page with a quotation or a message (optional). Inspire your readers with a relevant quotation or personal message.

- Dedication page (optional). You may wish to dedicate your book to your parents, partner, children... It adds a nice touch.

- Table of contents (Highly recommended)

- Foreword (optional). Ask someone who is an authority on the subject to write a few words about the book.

- Preface (optional). You can include a preface if you like, which may give the reader some background or insights into why you decided to write your book.

- Acknowledgments (optional). You may wish to thank certain people by name and can add this either at the beginning or end of your book.

The **back section** is the final pages of your book, once you have finished writing the main content and conclusion. You can choose which of the following you wish to add:

- Afterword (optional). You may wish to leave your readers with a closing statement or some parting words.

- Appendices (optional). Perhaps you had some graphs, charts, or diagrams that you didn't want to include in the main body of text. You can add them here.

- Glossary (optional). If you have a lot of technical or difficult terms that need further explanation, you can add a glossary for your readers' convenience.

- Index (optional). This is a time-consuming process so consider how useful it really is before you decide to do one.

• References or bibliography (optional). Whenever you use a quotation or citation from an external source, you should include the actual source/publication.

• Author bio (highly recommended). Let your readers learn more about you with a few paragraphs on your life, experience, skills, and goals.

• Follow or find me page (optional). If you have a website or social media platform for your book, ask readers to find you there by providing the correct links. You can also invite them to write a review for you on Amazon, now that they have read your book.

What else can I add?

A good nonfiction book includes lots of useful information. You are the expert but can still add interesting material from other sources to back up your content. You can quote experts, include the results of studies, and even refer to current events. With a mix of your own knowledge, personal anecdotes, and external sources, you are offering the audience a rich, credible, and engaging read.

How many chapters should I have?

That depends on you, although most nonfiction books will have at least five chapters and not more than fifteen. Less or more doesn't make you wrong, but it may seem weird to the reader, who is used to a certain number of chapters for books of this genre.

What software should I use?

Although most writers prefer to use pen and paper for a more organic experience, the truth is that we live in a digital world today. If you want to publish your nonfiction book on Amazon, you need to have it ready in digital form, which means the use of a pc, mac, or laptop.

Most of you will already be familiar with word processing software such as Microsoft Word or Google Docs. There are some differences between the two, but both are equally suitable. At this point, it is best to stick with whichever one feels the most familiar to you (we will get to editing and proofreading tools later on in the book).

There is also a range of book writing software available for online purchase that you may want to consider, depending on how much support you need in your writing and your experience level.

When you create an outline for your book, it will help you to focus on exactly what you want to say to the reader, and when. It is your roadmap and you can tweak it at any time if you wish to add or delete something, as long as you don't lose sight of your final destination.

In the following chapter, we are going to take a look at how to make sure you have a solid structure for your book. That means learning how to present each chapter in a logical, constructive way. If your ideas are all jumbled up, badly presented, or don't make sense, that will confuse your reader and make for a bad book.

A badly written book = bad/no reviews, fewer sales, and a blow to the ego.

Following a logical, well-laid-out sequence is the secret to holding the reader's attention, so that's exactly what we are going to investigate next.

❧ 5 ❧

CREATING THE STRUCTURE OF
YOUR BOOK

You have now nailed your nonfiction book outline and are probably raring to go. But, hold on for just one more minute. Have you thought about how it's going to be structured? If not, read on.

A lot of people rush to get their book finished without putting too much thought into what they are actually saying. Although it might make perfect sense to them while writing, the poor reader may find the content confusing, repetitive, or rambling.

Spending a little bit of time to think through how you want to present your ideas can make all the difference. It needs to be well organized – it needs structure.

If your book outline is your GPS to get you from A to B, your book structure is the actual car you are traveling in.

It's the chassis, the engine, and the four wheels that move the reader through the book. That's why it's so important to make sure it follows a logical sequence. But, how exactly do you create and craft that?

There's no standard formula – it all depends on the type of nonfiction book you are writing – but there are some tried and tested approaches you can take. I want to run through the different types of nonfiction books first, so you can be absolutely sure which category you fall into. Then, we'll look at ways to build a solid structure that your target audience can follow.

Types of nonfiction books

1. SELF-HELP

Many of you are probably intending to write a self-improvement or self-help book, such as this one. You can write about an enormous range of subjects, offering solutions to common problems that others may be facing. Whether you are writing about raising self-esteem or how to deal with acne, self-help books need to be informative and solution-oriented.

2. EXPOSÉ

This type of nonfiction book reveals or exposes the truth about a particular subject. You might want to take the lid off the fishing industry or shed light on the real events behind a cover-up. This kind of book can be tricky if you don't have intimate knowledge of the subject and can back up your arguments.

3. MEMOIR

Are you writing a historical account based on personal knowledge or from certain sources? Maybe you are telling the story of how your grandfather explored the Congo, or have done research into an achievement by a famous historical figure, such as Thomas Edison, and want to write about that.

4. AUTOBIOGRAPHY

Autobiographies are similar to memoirs, the difference being that instead of focusing on an aspect of someone else's life, you are retelling your own story. This is a popular subgenre for celebrities, influencers, or public figures who want to share their life story so far.

5. BIOGRAPHY

A biography is a book written by you about someone else and can be anyone that you are interested in. You can tell their story from your own perspective and even be creative about how you present the information. Their permission will be needed before you publish, of course.

6. NARRATIVE

This is a big subgenre and includes everything from creative nonfiction to long-form journalism. Narrative nonfiction is usually quite creative and may not even feel like nonfiction at all, but if it's intended to be taken as true, it definitely is. Some good examples could be writing about your life inside a cult or the year you spent in Tanzania with the Red Cross.

Knowing exactly which category you are intending to write about will not only help you decide WHAT to say but also HOW to say it.

Creating your structure

Depending on your book's subject, you can create different structures to make your work flow well. Think of it as building a car – what do you need to make it efficient, practical, and effective?

★ Follow a timeline

This makes a lot of sense if you are writing a biography or autobiography, and you simply tell the story through time. You can also use a timeline if you are writing a book about parenting, for instance, and want to refer to each stage of a child's life from infant to teenager.

★ Storytelling

You can tell a story even if it is nonfiction. Begin with the problem and work through the book until you reach a solution. If you want to write about management techniques, start by explaining the way things have traditionally been done before moving on to new approaches, with tips along the way for the reader to apply.

★ Step-by-step

The step-by-step approach is popular because it gives clearly defined advice for the reader to follow. If you want to teach your audience how to do something, each chapter can outline the information to be had. Whether you want to share with them how to build their own pc or lose weight easily, this kind of structure works really well.

★ By topic

If you want to write about a subject that has many sub-categories, let's say the wildlife in your area, you can divide the book up into sections such as mammals, sea life, birds, and insects, for example. This helps you to organize your writing and allows the reader to have a clear picture of what they will read about in each chapter.

When you have a lot of information that you want to put in your book, think about which structure is best for you and organize your thoughts in line with that.

You now have an idea about what category you fall into – so far, so good. But what about creating the structure for the actual chapters?

Every chapter of your book is one part of the whole machine and each deserves the same attention. They should all follow a similar pattern otherwise, your thoughts may come across as random, scatty, or inconsistent. The reader likes to feel that they are following a steady train of thought, not caught up in a tangled ball of string, which is why your chapters should be clearly titled and presented.

Your aim is to offer bite-sized chunks of information that are easily digestible and can be enjoyed in more than one sitting. Here are some answers to questions you may have about your chapter structure:

How long should each chapter be? There aren't any set rules and it depends on the topic of your nonfiction book. You can look at other books in the same niche as yours to find out what other writers are doing

A good rule of thumb is this:

30,000 word book = Introduction + 8 chapters + Conclusion

Introduction = 1-2,000 words

Conclusion = 1,000 words

Each chapter = approximately 3,300 words

This is only a guideline, but it does give you some idea of what length each chapter should be. You can add more chapters if you like, and tweak the word count accordingly, but it's entirely up to you. Estimate what you have to say and don't 'fluff up' content just to increase your word count – readers will spot that immediately.

If you aim to write a nonfiction book of around 50,000-70,000 words, you may wish to add more chapters, each one being anything from 3,500 to 5,000 words long. Some chapters may need more details and others less, depending on what you want to say. Focus on the quality of what you write, and worry later about how many words you have written.

What should I include in each chapter?

Each chapter should follow a similar format, which includes the following essential elements:

1. A catchy title or headline

2. An introduction that hooks the reader

3. A body of paragraphs that provide further details

4. A recap of the chapter

5. A transition to the next chapter

Your chapter title needs to be eye-catching. It's irrelevant how great your content is; if your chapter headline doesn't capture the attention, no one is going to read it. This is especially true when prospective buyers are skimming through the '*Look inside*' feature on your Amazon page, where they can see the table of contents.

Depending on your chosen genre and writing style, all your chapter contents should contain information related to your overall theme.

If any of the contents don't seem to fit your chapter's theme, remove it and think about where it will fit best - maybe in a chapter of its own, or added to a different one. Don't add anything that isn't useful to the reader.

Your Introduction should present the topic, say why you are writing this book, give the reader a taste of what they are about to read in a small summary, and end by making them feel that they should keep reading. If your introduction is boring or unclear, it will put the reader off from the word go, so spend some time thinking about WHAT you really want to say and WHY the audience should turn the next page.

For each individual chapter, one way to get your reader's interest in the first paragraph is to hook them in and make them want to read more. You can do this by asking a question, or making a surprising statement that spikes their interest.

It could be something like; *Do you find it difficult to manage your time?* Or, *Why being allergic to cats is a good thing.* Share a personal story or add a powerful quote that the reader can relate to, helping to build a connection from the offset.

If you are writing a self-help book, it's a good idea to talk about your own experience of the problem because that adds credibility and makes the reader feel that you know what you are talking about. With so many books out there on a similar subject, you have to ask yourself:

- Why should others listen to you?

- How is your story different?

- How can you help others?

- Do you really know what it feels like?

Write about your experiences, point out your mistakes, relate your journey, show what you have learned, be human – that's what readers are looking for.

When you gain your reader's trust, they will be more likely to listen to your advice. You can also tell them how different their lives will be once they finish reading your book, implement your strategies, use your products, and so on.

Expand on your story in each paragraph. This is where you give them what they have been looking for – the solutions to their problems. Add bullet points to make it more visually interesting, rather than writing long, complicated chunks of text that can be tiring to read. If you have noticed, throughout this book, each chapter has several points that are numbered or listed in some way so make sure to use them in your book to break up your content.

The last paragraph in the chapter should be a summary of what you have been talking about, leaving readers with the key takeaway that you wish to give them. Add a 'call to action', which asks them to take your advice or make them think about what they have just read. Finally, ease them into the next chapter with a few sentences on what is to follow.

Your final chapter, or Conclusion, can be a recap of all the main points of your book. It should remind readers of what they have learned and draw their attention to the main message you wanted to get across. Leave them with a sense of fulfillment and mention your next book, if you intend to write one. Include ways that they can contact you, such as joining your mailing list for more tips, and guide readers into your sales funnel for any courses or coaching that you may offer.

By following this formula for each chapter, you will be able to present a well-thought-out book that is interesting, useful, and easy to read. Essentially, it will be the vehicle that takes you smoothly to your final destination.

A word about writing style

The best way to present information and prove that you are an expert is to keep your writing as simple as possible. Complicated sentences and the use of jargon may make you feel clever, but if the audience finds it difficult to read, you are shooting yourself in the foot. Aim for readability, not making an impression, and you will get much more positive feedback from your fans through their reviews on your Amazon page.

If you are writing in English, make sure that you stick to the correct variant throughout your book. For example, when using American English, both spelling and punctuation should abide by the specific language rules, which are slightly different from British English. Don't use a mixture of both as this can be a distraction to the reader and may call your credibility into question.

Once you have completed all of your chapters, your manuscript is ready to be edited, proofread, and formatted. First-time writers are often confused about these next three steps and don't realize how important they are in getting their draft up to publishing standards.

This is a crucial part of the nonfiction book writing and publishing process, so pay very close attention to the next chapter – you will definitely learn from it!

❧ 6 ❧

EDITING, PROOFREADING & FORMATTING

Your manuscript is complete and you are happy with the results. You've covered everything that you wanted to say and are ready to move on to the next step of your publishing journey. But, you still have some way to go.

Let's face it; we didn't all pay attention in English class and aren't always sure if what we write is correct. It may seem Ok to you, but Ok is not good enough. You really need a good set of eyes to make sure that it is up to scratch and error-free before you think about putting it on Amazon.

Even the most accomplished writers/authors have their work checked and double-checked by a team of highly skilled editors. With self-publishing, you don't necessarily have that backup, but there are still things you can do yourself for little or no cost to make sure that what you have written holds up under scrutiny.

There's nothing worse than reading a book that has silly typos, awkward sentences, and bad punctuation. In addition, if the structure is wrong, doesn't flow well, or the formatting is inconsistent, you could end up with bad reviews and few sales. Apart from that, it's just unprofessional and can seriously damage your reputation as a writer.

There are three stages to getting your manuscript to a print-worthy state and these are:

Editing

Proofreading

Formatting

We are going to take a look at each one and I'll also give you some suggestions on different tools you can use to get the job done perfectly.

1. Editing

In the world of traditional publishing, you send your manuscript off to the publishing house, which has a team of editors specialized in reading book manuscripts. Now, with self-publishing being so popular, things are done differently, and it's down to you to do the editing of your book.

There are two types of editing – the first one is called 'developmental editing' and the other is 'line editing'. Basically, the first one means checking that your overall structure and content are sound, while the second one deals with the nitty-gritty of typos, punctuation, and so on. For the purposes of this book, I am going to give you some tips on how to do both, by knowing what to look out for and how to check if what you have written is correct or not.

❖ Read it through again

➢ As you read through each chapter, ask yourself if it contains information that is relevant to the chapter title. If not, consider taking out whatever is unrelated.

➢ What could you add to make it stronger?

➢ Do you explain any technical or complicated jargon that you use?

➢ Would the addition of sub-headings make any sections clearer?

➢ Are you getting your point across successfully or leading the reader into a maze?

❖ Cut out what you don't need

➢ On reading your manuscript again, it will become obvious if you are repeating yourself so don't be afraid to cut and snip where appropriate.

➢ Check your word count afterward and as long as the cuts you have made aren't too drastic, don't worry. If you do feel that you would like to increase the number of words, make sure that what you add is necessary and not just padding – readers will spot that.

❖ Do a fact check

➢ Make sure that any facts you mention are accurate by re-checking them. It's one thing to give your opinion and quite another to write something that just isn't true.

➢ What about any quotes or references that you use? Are they correct and have you mentioned the sources anywhere? (You can add footnotes at the bottom of each page or mention them at the end of your book in an Appendix.)

❖ Add paragraph transitions

➢ Help the reader to ease into each new paragraph by making sure you have used the right kind of words to allow for that. New paragraphs should begin with words or phrases that act as bridges for your ideas, such as the following examples:

Moreover,

Initially,

Here's the thing,

What's more,

So...

And yet,

In addition,

In contrast,

❖ Read out loud

➢ When you read your book out loud to yourself, you will be able to hear how good, or bad, it sounds. You may want to publish it as an audiobook at a later date, so this is a good check for both consistency, accuracy, and flow.

➢ There are also a lot of free text-to-speech extensions that you can download. They will 'read' your text for you so you can sit back and listen to it. You can even choose the gender of the 'reader' and the accent, such as Australian English.

❖ Rinse and repeat

➢ It may seem tedious now, but reading through your manuscript a couple of times is well worth it. You will come across things you have missed and it also helps you to be really certain that it includes what you want to say in a clear, organized, and interesting way.

2. Proofreading

Proofreading is quite a detailed task and you are looking for very specific things here. You aren't concerned with the content, but tiny things like comma use, italics, misspellings, and so on. Proofreading should ideally be carried out both before and after the formatting stage.

❖ How can you proofread your own work?

➢ At this point, you are checking for spelling mistakes, punctuation errors, correct word usage, line spacing, and fonts. Sometimes, this can feel like looking for a needle in a haystack so take your time and work through each chapter slowly.

➢ Use the grammar and spell-check of your software (be that MS Word, Pages, or Google Docs). This will catch any misspelled words and allow you to change them. It will also flag extra spaces in between words and wrong punctuation.

➢ There are plenty of free editing/proofreading software tools online that you can copy or upload your text to. You will then be given a list of suggestions about each word or phrase that may need changing. Caution is strongly advised here because these software programs use artificial intelligence, which isn't the same as a human brain (not just yet, anyway).

➢ Use the *find & replace* option on your software, or the *search*. If, for example, you want to check how many times you have used the word 'awesome', this function flags up that word and you can then decide if you have used it too much and change it to another word in some parts.

➢ We all have blind spots and often can't see our errors because it's us who wrote them in the first place and our brain tells us they are correct. You may make mistakes without realizing it, which is why it is a good idea to ask someone who you trust to also take a look at your manuscript.

➢ When you get stuck with issues like how to use capital letters, where to abbreviate, whether to use a colon or semi-colon, you can refer to a 'style guide'. These lay out the rules for a particular type of writing and include the Chicago Manual of Style (CMS) for American English, and its British equivalent, New Hart's Rules. You can also refer to any good dictionary, many of which are available online.

➢ If you really feel that you need expert help, there are thousands of professional proofreaders out there who you can hire to go through your manuscript. Prices tend to vary, depending on the size of your book and its difficulty level.

3. Formatting

There are two aspects of the formatting process.

The first one is making sure that your manuscript has been written in a consistent format throughout. You have probably created it with MS Word or Google Docs and it is important to make sure everything is streamlined to avoid problems later. The second stage of formatting relates to making sure it is suitable to upload on Amazon as a paperback or ebook because you can't export it directly without doing so first.

❖ Formatting for consistency

➢ Use black, 12-point, Times New Roman, or an equivalent font such as Calibri, Garamond, Georgia, or Arial.

➢ Don't use a fancy font for effect, no matter how tempted you are. It may not be recognized anyway by Kindle Create (see below) and can be overpowering for the reader after a while.

➢ MS Word and Google Docs have built-in page margins but if you are not sure, check that they are set at 1 inch on all sides.

➤ Set alignment to 'left justified'.

➤ Use a single space after periods/full stops.

➤ Use double-spaced line spacing.

➤ For nonfiction, you don't need to indent all paragraphs but you should leave a space between each one.

➤ Use page breaks when you want to begin a new chapter. Don't just keep hitting return, because you are creating 'invisible' spaces that will be difficult to get rid of later on.

➤ You don't need to number your pages. This will be done automatically when you format the manuscript for Amazon.

❖ **Formatting before uploading to Amazon.**

In order to successfully upload your manuscript to Amazon, it must be in an Amazon-friendly format. Below you will find the easiest ways to do just that.

➤ **Use Kindle Create.** This is Amazon's very own formatting app, designed especially for self-publishers. You can download it from Kindle Direct Publishing or KDP (part of the Amazon group). Simply import your manuscript once you have downloaded Kindle Create and the app will allow you to select certain styles, alter the typeset and tweak your manuscript. Once you are happy with the result, hit the publish button. The app then creates what is called a **.kdf file** for you to upload to KDP.

➤ **Use Vellum.** Vellum is the ultimate ebook formatting and layout tool for Mac users. To use Vellum, you first need to have your manuscript in a .docx format. Just like Kindle Create, Vellum has limited word processing capabilities, so make sure that your manuscript is ready for publishing. You can fully customize your book's setup, from the headings to block quotes or ornamental breaks, choosing the options that suit you best. You can also preview how your finished book will look on any device, such as a mobile phone or tablet. Vellum is not free, but offers various pricing packages, depending on your needs.

➢ **Other paying apps.** You will find other paying apps if you do a web search that can handle the formatting of your manuscript for you. Some work as a word processor too, so you can actually create your manuscript there, and then they do all the formatting, allowing you to export your doc in a variety of formats, such as ePub, and PDF.

➢ **Find a freelancer.** You may have thoroughly enjoyed writing your book but can't find the energy or time to do all of the formatting needed. There are plenty of reputable free-lancing platforms out there hosting professionals ready to handle your project for you. Prices can vary and some free-lancers are more experienced than others so read their profiles, look at their job success ratings and connect with them before deciding if they are suitable for you.

One useful tip is to print out a copy of your final draft or manuscript. You can then read through it and mark changes with a pen as you do so. This is a good way to spot any errors but it does mean that once you have detected mistakes or want to amend something, you need to go back to your digital copy and transfer the changes. It can be time-consuming, so it's not a 'must' but may prove useful.

You are nearly at the end of your publishing journey. You have written, edited, and proofread your whole book. You have formatted it and are ready to upload it to Amazon. Before you do so, spend some time proofreading your formatted file again to make sure that everything is correct. Often, text can disappear, be moved around, or spaces created where there shouldn't be any. If you have added images to your book, make sure they are positioned correctly and check that you are completely happy with the finished outcome. You can always change anything that you don't like.

Now, all that is left to do is to create your book cover and the 'blurb' to go on it. The design of your cover itself is something best left to the experts, and you can find out exactly what is involved in the next chapter.

HOW TO CREATE YOUR BOOK BLURB AND BOOK COVER

You can judge a book by its cover, and most people do when shopping on Amazon.

Your cover is what gets people interested enough in your book to consider buying it and that includes both the title, how visually eye-catching your front cover is, as well as what you write on the back.

Pick up any book and when you turn to the back, you will read some information about the contents. It's usually not more than 200 words or so, and may also include a small bio about the author. This is called the book 'blurb' and it's an essential part of your nonfiction book. People buying on Amazon can't pick up your book as they would in a normal bookstore and flick through the pages. They can use the 'look inside' feature to see your Table of Contents, the Introduction, and maybe a couple more pages, but that's about it.

Your book blurb is the information that will arouse their interest and want them to read more. It is the trailer for your book and the sales pitch to thousands of potential readers.

Your intention isn't to give a summary of the book, but to hook the reader in enough to make them want to buy it. The book blurb gives hints about what the reader can learn or discover but doesn't give the whole story away, so it's important to make sure that you get it right.

The typical process of discovery most readers will go through when they come across your book on Amazon is this:

• After doing an Amazon search, first of all, they will see your title and cover design.

• Then, they'll read the blurb as it appears on the Amazon book description that comes up when they click on your title link or your cover.

• Next, they'll use the 'look inside' feature to browse a few things in your Table of Contents

• Finally, they'll read your Introduction, which they can also find with the 'look inside' feature.

Unless the reader is specifically looking for your book, this is the marketing sequence a potential buyer will go through. They will, of course, probably read the reviews on the Amazon book page too, but they'll only do that when seriously considering whether to buy it or not.

When creating your book blurb, you have to bear in mind your target audience and a second audience: Amazon's search algorithm. If you click on a title or cover design on Amazon to view the listing, you only see the first paragraph in the blurb and a bit of the second, followed by a "Read More" prompt.

Obviously, you need to make that information as attractive as possible to get them to want to 'read more'. Whatever you write must contain those important keywords that readers will use when searching Amazon. This helps your book to appear in more searches and once they have found you, readers will read your book blurb and hopefully buy your book.

My 8 essential tips for creating a good book blurb are these:

1. Keep it short — 200-220 words is just about right

2. Write your blurb in the second person. Instead of using 'I', talk about yourself from another person's viewpoint, writing 'he' or 'she'.

3. Start your blurb with an open-ended question, such as, "Are you looking for the secret to success?"

4. Don't spill all the beans just yet. The reader will have to buy the book to learn more.

5. Write the blurb as if you were talking directly to one person. Instead of saying, "Everyone can learn something from this book," write, "You will unlock the secrets and find the answers to your problems..."

6. Specify what problem your reader may be experiencing.

7. Hint at how they can be solved.

8. Describe what the reader's future will look like after reading your book.

What your book blurb shouldn't do:

➜ Rely on clichés

➜ Make empty promises that can't be met

➜ Overly sensationalize the topic

➜ Reveal the secrets or plots

➜ Talk blatantly about how great the book is

Here's an example of a good book blurb for a new dieting book:

Book Title: *How to Lose 125 Pounds By Changing Your Mindset*

Back Cover Blurb:

Losing weight is hard and the more pounds you want to shed, the harder it can seem. Yo-yo diets, fasting, here today and gone tomorrow food fads all make the dieting game feel like an uphill struggle. This book comes to end all that, with its emphasis on changing your mindset before thinking about changing what you eat. Its innovative content will get you to rethink your whole approach to food and work from the inside out, helping you to create a new weight-loss mindset. The writer will talk you through the importance of healthy thought patterns, provide strategies for creating daily habits that discipline your cravings, and help you to become more conscious of your food intake. You'll also find some delicious, easy-to-prepare recipes that will feed both your body and soul.

Forget about 'having' to follow a strict diet and focus instead on your inner wellbeing. With a range of tried and tested strategies for effective weight loss that are both practical and economical, the author gives you the tools to see food from a different perspective. Meal plans based on your needs instead of what the weighing scales say can be found within, as well as exercises on how to be more mindful about your body.

This book is a game-changer when it comes to weight loss and will convert you from a die-hard dieter to a healthier you, both inside and out!

This blurb is 236 words. If I wanted to cut it down to 220, I would but it isn't really necessary. It's Ok to break some small rules now and again!

By following my 8 essential tips, you can write a successful back cover blurb that acts as a critical point of communication when you promote your book.

If you get stuck writing your blurb, you can always hire an editor to help you develop your ideas. Find someone who has experience with the ins and outs of publishing and learn what you can from them. You can also look at book blurbs on other books in the same genre as yours to see what they include and to get some ideas.

Creating the ideal book cover

Writers often reach a huge stumbling block when it comes to creating their book cover. They usually have no skills related to this aspect of self-publishing and don't know where to turn. It can be very overwhelming and frustrating, not to mention expensive if you hire a top-notch graphic designer to do it for you.

Let's work through this stage of finalizing your complete book and look at your options for creating an engaging cover that makes your target reader want to buy it.

Do it yourself

1. If you have your book title and a concept for your cover, that's a great start. Even at this late stage in the game, many self-publishing authors still haven't decided on the title or thought about what their cover will look like. You need to do this **NOW**!

2. Download a book cover template from Amazon by typing in **kdp cover template** in your browser. This will take you to the KDP page for Paperback Cover Templates. You need to select your trim size, the number of pages your book will have, and the color of the paper before downloading the correct template to your pc. The most commonly used trim

size for nonfiction books is 5" x 8" (12.7 x 20.32 cm) or 6" x 9" (15.24 x 22.86 cm).

3. Now that you have a template to work with, you can go over to **canva.com**, which is a free platform for digital creations. (It does offer a premium service but you don't really need that.) Once there, you can upload your template and begin to create your design after you have entered the correct dimensions. Play around with the different fonts and other available tools until you are happy.

4. Your front cover should include your book title, possibly a sub-title, and your author name. Your back cover should include your book blurb and a small author bio if you like.

5. You can upload your own image for the book cover, or choose from a selection of free images on canva. As long as you are legally entitled to use the image or it is free for use in the public domain, you are fine.

6. When you are done, simply save your book cover and download it as **PDF Print high quality.** It is then ready to upload onto Amazon when you get to the publishing stage.

7. Note: If you want to create an ebook cover too, this should be the same design as your paperback but without the back part. When you upload it to Amazon, make sure it is in **TIFF (.tif/.tiff) or JPEG (.jpeg/.jpg) format.**

8. There are similar platforms with ready-made book template ideas that usually have a basic free service and offer more advanced options in their paid packages. Adobe Spark and EDIT.org, are just two examples.

Hire a professional

If you really don't want to bother with the book cover process, there are plenty of professionals out there willing to help you. You will also find a range of online options that offer this service for a fee.

1. Find a freelancer. There are thousands of freelance graphic designers and book cover illustrators who can produce a professional-looking cover for your book. Platforms such as Fiverr and Upwork are great places to look as you can check out freelancer portfolios and see their price ranges. Once you connect with someone, they can send you samples of covers and, of course, you can direct them on what you have in mind or leave them to come up with something original for you.

2. Subscribe to online services such as 99 designs for a flat fee and run a competition. More than a million freelancers are available to make a bid once you have indicated the design requirements for your book. You can then choose the winning cover from those submitted.

The options for finding someone to design the cover for your book are by no means exhaustive. What I would point out are the following useful tips:

★ You get what you pay for. The lower the cost, the less experience and expertise the designer probably has.

★ Budget is always a concern, so it's important to shop around and see what you can stretch to. You can pay anything from £30 ($40) to £800 ($1000) depending on what is involved.

★ You MUST tell your chosen designer from the start that you are intending to self-publish on Amazon. This affects how they will create your cover and the format you will receive the final version in.

★ If this is your first book, you want to make a good impression. While the idea of creating the cover yourself for free may seem tempting, ask yourself if you really have what it takes to assess what is a good or bad cover.

★ No matter what cover you would 'like' to create, think about how relevant it is to your target audience. Does it convey what you want to say? Is it attractive? Is it clear? Would you buy that book, based on its cover?

One advantage of self-publishing on Amazon is that your book is also allocated an ISBN (International Standard Book Number). You can find these on the back of all books – a series of 13-digits or less in a small barcode box. If you plan to eventually sell your book on other platforms too, you need to buy your own ISBN. During the uploading process, KDP will ask you if you already have an ISBN and if so, you can add it to the relevant field.

Uploading your book onto the KDP website is a very easy process. Remember that you will need two covers: one front-back cover for your paperback version in PDF format, and a separate front-only cover in JPEG format for your ebook version.

So, there you have it! Your manuscript is polished and your book cover with blurb is all set up. This is the exciting moment you have been waiting for – time to press that PUBLISH button.

Hopefully, everything goes to plan and your nonfiction book takes pride of place on the Amazon bookshelves. All that is left to do now is promote it to the world. I can already hear you asking how on earth you are supposed to do that, which is why I am including a bonus chapter on that exact subject!

❧ 8 ❧

BOOK PROMOTION SECRETS

I t's a great feeling to see your finished book available on Amazon. You will probably order some author copies and tell your friends, family, and colleagues about it, hoping they will buy it.

That's a nice move, but it's not enough to generate real sales. And, unfortunately, unless you are a celebrity or already well-known, no one else is going to purposefully look for your book and buy it. So what now?

You need a marketing strategy that will be directed at your target audience and you should cast a wide net. Telling your friends about it on Facebook isn't the only thing you can do — there are many other ways to market your nonfiction book, which I will explain below.

As the world is becoming more digital, online book promotion must be a key aspect of your marketing strategy. The more exposure you get on web-based platforms, the better. Some of the marketing strategies can be time-consuming and you must be prepared to put in the work if you want to see any results.

Before you begin, you need to consider where your target audience is and think about your potential readers.

- Where do they look for new books?

- Which social media platforms do they use?

- Who do they follow? (publishers, writers, book reviews...)

- What keywords will they type into an online search?

- What images and graphics will draw their attention to your book?

- What other nonfiction books on similar topics are they buying?

- Who are your competitors, and what are they doing?

Once you've done your research, this will give you a clearer picture of where your readers 'hang out' and what they buy.

You need a strong online presence to establish yourself as a professional nonfiction writer and the internet must be a large part of your book marketing plan. Everyone uses the internet, from checking their social media accounts to reading blogs, researching products, and watching YouTube videos. Taking advantage of that fact is therefore crucial. It's your chance to tell the world about your book. Think of it this way:

- In 2021, there are currently **4.66 billion** active internet users worldwide.

- **65.6%** of the entire world's population has internet access.

- Internet users spend an average of **6 hours and 56 minutes** online every day.

- **Eight out of every ten** US adults go online daily.

- Revenues from e-commerce retail were projected to hit **$4.2 trillion** in 2020.

- Each month, more than **197 million** people around the world visit Amazon.com.

- In 2016, it is estimated that self-published books made up around **60%** of the ebooks offered on Kindle Unlimited by Amazon.com

- Audible, a subsidiary of Amazon.com, is the largest audiobook producer and retailer in North America and offers over **100,000 unique titles**.

Despite Amazon being criticized by traditional publishing companies for having too much leverage and influence in the market, there's no denying that it is still the place to be if you want to self-publish. There are other platforms, but for the purpose of this book, we are looking at Amazon as your shop window.

When visitors stop at your shop window, they see your book cover and may read your book description, as well as using the look inside feature. But you have to get them to find your 'shop' first. With millions of books already on Amazon, how do you get people to find yours?

There are two ways to do this and my suggestion is that you use both. The way you market your book will depend on your budget and there are also free options if budget is an issue for you at this time.

Type 1. Passive Marketing. (This will also involve paid advertising.)

As you are selling on Amazon, let's start with Amazon Ads.

1. Create a campaign using either automatic targeting or manual targeting. With automatic targeting, Amazon chooses

the keywords to target your book on the Amazon platform. With manual targeting, you choose which keywords to use so people on Amazon can find you.

2. You will pay a certain amount per click (this means that every time someone clicks on your book, you will pay a small amount.)

3. Amazon will make a suggestion on how much you should pay per click and you can adjust the price up or down. Obviously, the less you bid, the less your ad will be seen.

4. Keywords are simply words that people type in the Amazon search bar to find books just like yours. Your main topic, for example, *Self-Help For First Time Home Owners*, (the title of your book) will have many related keywords that people type in every day.

5. To find out which keywords to use in your ad, there are a variety of options:

a. Type your main keyword into the search bar. As you do so, related keywords will start to appear under the search term. Choose some or all of them for your advertising campaign.

b. Use a free keyword tool like Semrush. You don't need to buy the paid version, which is very expensive. You can input up to five keyword ideas a day for free. This tool will also show you related keywords and how many monthly searches that keyword gets on the internet.

c. For a more advanced keyword search, you can opt for a paid service such as **KDSPY.** This is a plugin tool that focuses your keyword research on the data available on the Kindle Book Store. You can install it and access the information you need with one click.

You can also use other paid advertising platforms, such as BookBub ads. This allows you to create your own display ads and a cover picture of your book. It only includes ads for ebooks and Audible books at the moment but creates a direct link back to Amazon so your buyer on Bookbub buys from your Amazon ad.

TYPE 2. ACTIVE MARKETING.

Here, we are mainly talking about free marketing. There may be some small costs, but they won't break the bank. I would recommend you begin with active marketing first. Once your books have at least 10 reviews on your Amazon page, then you might want to invest some money in advertising. But you don't really want to be sending paid ads to books that have zero reviews.

Active marketing takes time but is an effective way to get your book known and a good foundation on which to build a profitable self-publishing business. If you don't feel up to the challenge of marketing your book yourself, you can hire a marketing expert to do that for you. Obviously, this increases the cost, but you may consider it as an option after thinking about the time you will need to spend yourself and your level of expertise.

HERE ARE SOME NO, OR LOW-COST IDEAS:

1. Facebook. Love it or loathe it, you can't get away from the fact that approximately 2.85 billion people are members (2021). People spend a fair bit of time there each and every day. If you already have a Facebook account yourself, you can create an Author Page where you showcase your book. You can also arrange for highly targeted paid advertising on Facebook and get useful data on how successful your ad campaign was, for as little as $5 a day.

a. Create a Facebook Group **before** you launch your book. Create the group in the niche of your book and invite people interested in that theme to join. The correct way to do this is to join other groups in that niche and become friends with their members. Then, invite them to your group.

b. In the first 30 days of launching your book on Amazon, it is very important that the Amazon algorithm sees some movement on your book. You need reviews and you need them quickly. There are many people you can share your book with to get reviews, both on your Author Page and Facebook Group.

c. When people join your group, make it clear in the questions asked to all new members that you will sometimes be giving away a free book in return for a review. Don't incentivize reviews, just ask people. Message them personally every time you have a book coming out. Give them the digital version of your book, with a link to the review page on Amazon, and allow them some time to read the book before you get back to them a week or so later

d. Here is a sample of a review request that you can send:

Re: Respectful request for a review of my latest book "Love Yourself Deeply"

Hi,

I know you are super busy.

I would love to give you a copy of my latest book in return for your valued opinion.

It's called "Love Yourself Deeply" and currently sells for around $14 on Amazon.

It's 138 pages long and is packed with ideas on how to feel better about yourself as a woman by overcoming low self-esteem, low self-confidence, and low self-worth.

You may not suffer from any of those things yourself, but many women do.

The author overcame these negative traits herself to become the self-confident businesswoman she is today.

I hope you can find time in your schedule to review it

Reviews are the lifeblood of a book, especially in the early days. More reviews = more readers and that helps myself and my female writer to create more books for you.

Your review would help us out no end.

Please let me know.

All the best, Keith

e. Don't forget to post good quality information daily on your Facebook Group to keep people interested. You want them to drop by each and every day and they won't do that if your posts are boring, repetitive, or uninspiring. Give them interesting content in the form of blog posts (yours or other people's) and even drop snippets from your book in there. I generally give people two or three paragraphs.

2. Create a blog, or use your existing blog. This is a good way for you to keep your writing routine active and to regularly promote your book's subject matter.

a. Link your book's Amazon page to each blog post, so they can find it easily without having to do a search. I also create some banner ads for each book. People do actually click on these and some will buy.

b. Concentrate on getting traffic to your blog. You can do this by posting your blog posts on your social media accounts and your Facebook Group. I also create video tips on my YouTube channel and have links underneath to my books and blog.

3. Email Marketing. This is a very important part of promoting your book and you should build an email list before you have actually published it.

a. There are many software options on the market that you can use to create an email list and generate those emails for your target audience. I use an autoresponder from Get Response. This works out at around $20 a month. The software delivers a sequence of emails to the people on my list in the correct order. You can call them newsletters or promotions that are sent out regularly to people on your mailing list.

b. You can market your books and ask for reviews via email. I would suggest creating an incentive for them to join your list, such as a free report. Ideally, this should be a brief document that is on the same topic as your books.

c. You can add links to your book, your blog, and your Facebook Group in this free report.

d. Again, give people value. Deliver good content each day and include posts from your blog in the emails. Don't just sell to people or ask for reviews – they will soon unsubscribe. Keep people happy and they will keep opening your emails.

e. When someone buys your book, make sure you get them to sign up for your newsletter. If a reader doesn't end up on your mailing list, you won't be able to reach them when you have something else to sell (such as your next book).

4. Create a website. A professional-looking website is something you should definitely consider building.

a. It allows people to find out more about you and your books. It's also a hub where you can get readers to sign up to your mailing list with a pop-up box.

b. Here again, you can encourage them to give their email details if you offer them something in return, such as a report or a free book.

c. Although the thought of creating your own website may be daunting, you can find many self-service web design apps today that make the whole procedure extremely simple and for a low annual cost. Some of them also provide tools for creating your email content, or Lead Magnets (the free promotional stuff). If you still feel unsure, you can always hire a professional web designer to handle the setup of your website.

d. You can also write blogs on your website, and share them on your social media platforms.

I hope that I have given you some useful ideas on how to go about promoting your book. The time and effort that you put into it will definitely pay off and the more you learn, the more effective you will become. It's an ongoing process and you need to be on your game, but the end result is more sales of your book for little or no cost.

You are also creating a ready-made audience for the next book that you decide to write. Now that you have read this book and discovered how to do it, there's nothing stopping you.

Good luck and see you on Amazon!

CONCLUSION

When I first started writing this book, I wanted to create a step-by-step manual or roadmap for those new to the nonfiction self-publishing industry. It's something that I would have loved to have my hands on when I wrote my first book, **Money Mind Crush**.

During that time, I carried out hours of research on the best ways to write, publish and promote my book. I then went on to successfully publish my second book, **Awesome Kindle Book Ideas**, having the benefit of greater knowledge and insight into the whole process.

Like I said in the Introduction, I know that many people are thinking of self-publishing but have a lot of question marks on how to go about it. They see others doing it and think they must have some kind of superpowers or specialist intel. That's not true. Most first time self-published writers have probably lost a lot of time (and possibly money) as they struggled to get from the writing to publishing stage, and faced many hurdles along the way.

I wanted to write a book that shows you how to avoid the above potholes, and hope that I have accomplished that. Throughout these chapters, you will have found concise, easy-to-follow advice on what to write, how to write it, and how to self-publish and generate sales.

I hope you have enjoyed learning about how you too can write a nonfiction book as we debunked the idea that you have to be a certified 'expert' or skilled writer to do so. Knowing that there is a niche for everyone will hopefully help you to find out which one is best for you, and there is a lot of advice in this book on how to use search tools to discover just that.

I have included many examples of where to find inspiration for your book and ways to narrow down who will actually be interested in reading it. We don't all set off to write a book for a specific audience, so I hope that you have come to understand more about identifying your genre, which plays an important role when you go on to promote your finished book.

One of the difficulties that many of you will find when beginning your book-writing journey is knowing how to create a sound book outline and structure. Chapters 4 and 5 went into some detail about the two, explaining how to create a solid chapter framework and what to include in each one.

Learning how to catch and correct errors in your writing is also an essential part of the book writing process, and I have included a range of useful tips on how to handle the editing and proofreading side of it. This is the thing that sells – your content. Of course, preparing your final draft in a format that is Amazon-friendly is one of the stages of self-publishing that can cause a lot of headaches. I am confident that you found all of the information that you will need here to do so with great success.

Having an appealing cover and catchy title helps to sell your book, and you will have found plenty of insider information on how to achieve that, as well as a detailed look at how to create your bulletproof book blurb. Finally, you will have found some useful advice on how to promote your book on Amazon, as well as strategies for gaining maximum exposure on your social media accounts and other online platforms.

Most of the information in this book relates to how you can write and publish your first nonfiction book on Amazon with little or no extra cost. I have mentioned a variety of sources that can help you to get things done if you don't feel able to handle them yourself, such as paid software, apps, and free-lancer options. By all means, use professional help if you feel that you need it and can budget for it.

My wish for you is that, after reading this book, you will be in a better position to pursue your dream of writing, publishing, and promoting your first nonfiction book successfully on Amazon.

As you build up your confidence during the whole process, hopefully, you will also learn new skills, discover your hidden talents, and enjoy a great sense of accomplishment at the end of it all.

Before you know it, you will be ready to begin book number two.

Enjoy your self-publishing journey and thank you for reading!

One last word before you go...

Did you enjoy this book?

Your feedback helps me to provide the best quality books and also helps other readers like yourself to discover great books.

It would mean the world to me if you took just two minutes to share your thoughts about this book in a review on Amazon. Just type the name of the book into the Amazon search bar and leave your review.

Thanks in advance, Keith

SOURCES

FTC Disclosure, some links in this book contain affiliate links. This means that the Author/Publisher will receive some compensation in the form of commission from the sale of the product.

Amazon Ads

https://advertising.amazon.com/lp/grow-your-business-with-sponsored-ads

Chicago Manual of Style

New Hart's Rules, Oxford University Press, 201

https://www.chicagomanualofstyle.org/home.html

Vellum

https://keitheverett.co.uk/vellum

Semrush

https://www.semrush.com/analytics/keywordmagic/start

KDSPY

https://keitheverett.co.uk/kdspy1

BookBub

https://partners.bookbub.com/

GetResponse

https://keitheverett.co.uk/getresponse

Printed by BoD™in Norderstedt, Germany

9 781919 611273